James Gairdner, Petrus Carmelianus

The Camden Miscellany

Volume the Ninth

James Gairdner, Petrus Carmelianus

The Camden Miscellany
Volume the Ninth

ISBN/EAN: 9783337165574

Printed in Europe, USA, Canada, Australia, Japan

Cover: Foto ©Lupo / pixelio.de

More available books at **www.hansebooks.com**

"THE SPOUSELLS" OF THE PRINCESS MARY

DAUGHTER OF HENRY VII.,

TO

CHARLES PRINCE OF CASTILE,

A.D. 1508.

FIRST PRINTED BY PYNSON IN TWO EDITIONS,
ENGLISH AND LATIN.

EDITED FROM UNIQUE COPIES

BY

JAMES GAIRDNER.

PRINTED FOR THE CAMDEN SOCIETY.

M.DCCC.XCIII.

PREFACE.

In the year 1814 Mr., afterwards Sir Henry, Ellis called the attention of the Society of Antiquaries to an English tract printed by Pynson, of which a unique and fragmentary copy existed in the British Museum, giving an account of a really remarkable event in the end of Henry VII.'s reign, of which very little notice had been taken by historians. This was the reception of an embassy from the Emperor Maximilian to make a final conclusion, so far as diplomacy could do so, of the marriage already negociated between Henry's daughter Mary, said to be then about eleven years old (though I am afraid she was a little older)[a] with Maximilian's grandson, Charles Prince of Castile, a boy in his ninth year, who ultimately became the renowned Emperor Charles V. Of the contents of this tract, or of the portions then extant, Mr. Ellis gave a pretty full description, accompanied by copious extracts, in a letter to Mr. Samuel Lysons, which was printed in the eighteenth volume of the *Archæologia*; and in 1818 the whole of the existing text was reproduced in lithographic facsimile by the Roxburghe Club. Such an interesting typographical curiosity, illustrated as it was by two woodcuts—the one a frontispiece, the other a colophon with Pynson's mark and an ornamental border—seemed well to

[a] See note as to Mary's age at the end of this Preface.

deserve reproduction by lithography. The unique original copy
had certainly been maltreated ; the existing leaves were slightly
mutilated, and from the stain upon the margin they seemed to have
been used for the interior of a book-cover. The original remains
to this day a very imperfect copy ; but one leaf of the lost portion
has since been recovered, and, having been purchased by the British
Museum from the Trustees of Canon Greenwell in 1885, it is now
inserted in the tract.

A narrative of such a description printed by Richard Pynson
must of course have been published by authority; but Ellis was
not aware that it was published at the time in Latin as well as in
English. Nor would the fact be readily discovered even now by
searching book catalogues under the name of Mary or of Charles;
for the Latin edition did not bear either name upon the title page.
The existing copy in the Grenville library appears to be perfect;
and the only title that it bears is "Petri Carmeliani Carmen,"
which is merely that of the introductory poem.[a] It is most
sumptuously printed upon vellum in a rather larger type than the
main text of the English, and illustrated with four woodcuts, two of
which are identical in design with those which adorn the English
edition, but are finer in execution.[b] The other two were probably
not included in the English edition at all; both the beginning and
the end of the English tract are perfect, and though there is no
pagination, it is pretty certain from the signatures of the sheets

---

[a] It seemed to me at first that a title page must have preceded the prefatory poem
and been lost ; but the leaf which contains the poem is clearly the first leaf of the
first sheet, the next leaf bearing the signature A ii. This, in the opinion of Mr.
Graves of the British Museum, proves that there could have been no general title-
page. The title prefixed in this Edition, "Solennes Ceremoniæ et Triumphi," is
borrowed from the text. See page 2.

[b] The two sections of the lower part of the frontispiece may be from the same
blocks in both editions ; but the higher part, though the design corresponds in the
minutest details, is much coarser work in the English edition than in the Latin.

that the text, apart from the title page and colophon, extended only to twenty-three pages; while the Latin, omitting the illustrations, the title page, and the poem at the end, to which there is nothing corresponding in the English, amounts actually to forty-three pages. Now, though the exact proportion varies in different parts of the narrative, a page of the English, which is, with the exception of the first paragraph, in a smaller type than the Latin throughout, generally contains all but a few lines less than the matter contained in two pages of the other. It would seem, therefore, that the twenty-three pages of the English tract must have been fully occupied by letterpress, and that there was no room for the two other illustrations.

The Latin, therefore, was the finer and more sumptuous edition of the two, being intended for the use of a more refined and highly-educated public, abroad, no doubt, as well as at home. The English, which was probably translated from the other (for it does not strike me as being the original), was most likely a cheap edition to gladden the hearts of Henry's own loyal subjects. The text of the Latin, like the prefatory poem and the poetical epilogue by which it was accompanied, was probably the work of Peter Carmelianus, Henry VII.'s Latin Secretary.

The original frontispiece prefixed to both editions of this tract has been drawn and engraved on wood by my friend Mr. Ebsworth, who had generously offered to make drawings of the three other woodcuts also and engrave them himself for this edition. Unhappily his state of health has prevented him from fulfilling this intention, and the reader must now be satisfied with the descriptions of the other woodcuts given by the Editor in the places where they occur in the text.

It will be seen that the two tracts are printed here on the same pages, one above the other, so as to enable the reader easily to

compare the two. The translation is on the whole pretty close, but there are parts where the Latin gives somewhat fuller details than the English, as, for instance, at pp. 28—31, where the English, although the text is perfect here, omits altogether the substance of some paragraphs, and condenses others so much that it only gives a single page to what occupies four pages in the Latin edition.

So much for the form of these original documents, and for what concerns the editing. It remains to say a word or two about their substance and historical value. To the modern reader it may perhaps appear that their contents are little more than a flourish of trumpets over an ambitious project which led to no result. And it is true the project itself was in a few years set aside. The future of Europe was not actually shaped in accordance with the patient and skilful diplomacy which seemed to be crowned with such brilliant success in December, 1508. But if we are to dismiss from the page of history, as unworthy of serious attention, all the projects which have ended in smoke, we shall take pretty nearly the whole life out of the record. The things for which men strove (whether statesmen or common men) deserve, surely, quite as much attention in history as the things which they accomplished.

The "espousal," or, as we may call it, the betrothal of his daughter Mary to young Charlés, Prince of Castile, was a master-stroke of Henry the Seventh's policy achieved at the very end of his reign—only four months, in fact, before his death. It was not altogether without important results during the five years follow-ing, and it was really a far more wholesome piece of business in itself than what the other leading powers of Europe were nego-tiating during that very month of December at Cambray. Partly, no doubt, it was a move of Henry, with a view to pay off old scores against Ferdinand of Arragon, who, though still an ally, had

treated him very badly. But the main object was to increase the power and influence of England all over Europe, and secure for the King of England's daughter a most enviable position by allying her with a young prince, the possibility of whose succession to a large number of rich and important kingdoms was even then quite visible to the eye of a politician.

The uncertain thing about it, of course, was whether the House of Austria could be relied on to fulfil its engagements. But these were made as binding in the meantime as such engagements could be ; and the mere prestige of what was actually done was a considerable guarantee for its ultimate completion. The eyes of Europe were dazzled by the alliance, and when the ambassadors came and Lord Berghes as the proxy for the young prince actually set the ring upon the finger of the girlish bride, England really seemed to have taken quite a new position in the world. The Red Rose of the Tudors, to use the flowery simile of the narrator, now bloomed in Imperial gardens; and whatever statesmen, who knew its secrets, may have thought of the glory of the Holy Roman Empire, it is certain that it had a powerful influence still on the popular imagination.

The Emperor Maximilian, indeed, was unsteady enough, and Henry was undoubtedly aware that all the securities taken would have been quite insufficient to hold him to his engagements if at any time hereafter more tempting offers were held out to him elsewhere. But for the present there was no fear. Always in want of money, and not least so now when bewitched by France into a league for the spoliation of Venice, he looked to Henry as a money lender and pledged to him a valuable jewel for 50,000 crowns. Henry, who had warned Venice beforehand of her danger, had no sympathy with the plot which his other allies were hatching, and did not expect Maximilian to reap much profit from it ;

there were too many other freebooters engaged, far more sharp-sighted than the Emperor. But he had a plan of his own to suggest that would do Maximilian good and himself too. Maxi-milian, if he played his cards judiciously, might use his new friend-ship with France to cool that which had lately sprung up between France and Arragon, and then he could effectually demand of Ferdinand the government of Castile, in right of his grandson Charles. This was the policy which Henry was secretly urging Maximilian to pursue, and it is a curious question whether the English King, if he had lived but a few years longer, would not have succeeded in using the Emperor as an automaton to wrest the government of Castile from Ferdinand and to govern it himself.[a]

That such was Henry's intention there can be very little doubt ; and Ferdinand very well knew that it was his intention, though Englishmen at home were profoundly ignorant of it, and have remained so almost ever since. Lord Bacon, indeed, in his History of Henry VII., says that this was "a tradition in Spain though not with us," and he evidently thinks it not at all improbable, though later historians have passed over the matter in silence. But the diplomatic records brought to light in our day have made the matter certain ; and the following extract from a ciphered despatch of John Style, Henry VII.'s ambassador in Spain, will show how well Henry had studied the situation, and how valuable the little treatise we are discussing was in promoting the object that he had in view. Style's English, it is true, is a little uncouth, but there is no mistake about his meaning :—

" And it please your Grace, I delivered unto the King of Arragon the copy written in Latin of the noble triumph of the noble marriage of my lady Mary your noble daughter and the Prince of Castile. The King commanded Almaçan to copy it into Castelyns ; howbe that your Grace may be right well insured that it is much more displeasure to the King

[a] See my Letters and Papers, Ric. III. and Henry VII., i. 360-1.

and all his affinity than comfort to hear of the said noble marriage ; insomuch, and it please your Grace, that they say and will not believe that the said excellent marriage is so concluded. And the true Castilians, as the Great Captain,[a] and many other, to whom I have given copies written in Castilian, they do believe it, and take great rejoicing therein, and thereby they do trust for to have right much succour and comfort. And as to the said Great Captain, as by my other letters of late, I have certified unto your Highness that he was determined for to do his service unto your Grace and unto the Emperor, and in the right and favor of the Prince of Castile, his natural lord ; how be that the saying of the said Duke[b] is, and it please your Grace, that he of late considereth the great slackness that is in the Emperor in many ways, saying that it is nearby a whole year that a servant of his hath been in the Emperor's court for to know his pleasure, of the which he can have none answer; the which putteth him in great fear how that he and his company should be entreated in case that he and they came thither. And also he sayeth that he saith not what service that he should do in that parts, unless that the Prince's coming should be hitherwards shortly. That notwithstanding the said Duke's saying is that in case that your Highness shall please for to command him, or the Emperor or the Prince's Council will write unto him, assuring him that he shall be by them entertained and entreated to his honor, that then immediately he will repair unto them with all diligence to him possible, the which he may not do without great danger or jeopardy of the losing of a great part of his goods here, and all the lands that he hath in the realm of Naples ; for in case so were that the said Duke were departed from hence, all this land should be in trouble and his friends ; how be that, and it please your Grace, that no man's departing from this land may be more to the comfort of the Prince and to the displeasure of the King of Arragon than this Great Captain, the which as yet he, nother his friends, have not been favorably dealt withal by the King of Arragon. How be that, and it please your Grace, now daily I understand that the King

---

[a] Gonsalvo Fernandez of Cordova.
[b] Gonsalvo had the title of Duke of Terranova. See Calendar of State Papers of Henry VIII., Vol. I., No. 3593, at the end of Style's despatch.

maketh means to the said Great Captain and to the Marquis de Plego, the Count de Cabra, and other, for to have them incline unto him; the which I fear me that they will so do of very necessity, unless that they shall shortly have other comfort from your Highness and from the Emperor and the Prince's Council. As unto the Marquis de Villena and the Count de Benavente, the King hath rewarded them with great rents, so, and it please your Grace, that the said Marquis and Count do continue in this Court with the King, how be that trust his Highness hath none unto the said Marquis. Many great estates be well minded to the Prince, but in especial the Duke de Najara and the Count de Miranda, and in no wise there can no man be suffered to pass into Flanders; for many lords, gentlemen, and other would depart in case that they might pass, and such as that be taken going or coming from the Prince be sore prisoned without favor.

"Your Grace may be well insured that the King of Arragon is sore displeased with the conclusion of the marriage of the Prince of Castile, and so the bishop Don Pedro said unto me in secret that the King his lord had reason so for to be discontented, seeing the Prince which that should be his inheritor for to be married without his assent, the said bishop saying it would grieve a poor man for to see his inheritor for to be married without his assent, and much more a great prince as that the King my lord is."[a]

Ferdinand was relieved from many apprehensions by the death of the astute king who had made this dangerous move against him. Henry VIII. succeeded his father and established at once better terms with Spain by marrying Katharine of Arragon. But the marriage of Charles of Castile with Mary was not dropped. Ferdinand, indeed, did not love it much better than before, but he agreed to ratify it, and not only told the English ambassador that he was entirely satisfied with it, but promised to make his satisfaction publicly known in Spain.[b] How could he do otherwise?

[a] Memorials of Henry VII. (Rolls Series), pp. 438—440.
[b] Calendar of Henry VIII., Vol. I., Nos. 27, 240, 490 (p. 68).

The thing had gone too far not to be frankly recognised. Not only had the proxy marriage been effected, but the young bridegroom had actually written to Mary calling her his wife, and to her father calling him his father, and to her brother calling him his brother. So far, we are told (see pages 33, 34), Charles had actually committed himself, or rather been committed (for it must be remembered he was not yet nine years old), soon after the return of the embassy; and though the letters to Henry VII. are not extant, nor to his son Prince Henry, there is one to Mary herself which seems to have been written, not after the return of the embassy in December 1508, but while it was yet in England. It is couched in the following terms :—

CHARLES OF CASTILE TO THE PRINCESS MARY.

Ma bonne compaigne, le plus cordialement que je puis a v[ostre] bonne grace me recommande. Jay charge le Sieur de Bergh[ez] et autres mes ambassadeurs ordonnez par de la vous deviser [de la] disposition de ma personne et de mes affaires, vous priant l[es] vouloir croire et par eulx me faire savoir de vostre santé [et autres] bonnes nouvelles, qui est la chose que plus je desire, c[omme] scet le benoit Filz de Dieu, auquel je prie, ma bonne com[paigne], vous donner par sa grace ce que desirez. A Malines, [ce] xviij⁰ jour de decembre.

Vostro bon mary
(Signed) CHARLES.
(Countersigned) P. HANETO[N]
(Addressed) : A dame Marie ma bonne compaigne.*

This letter has been hitherto attributed to the year 1513 and is noticed under that date in the Calendar of State Papers of Henry VIII., Vol. I., No. 4606. Even in that case it is the earliest letter extant (so far as I am aware) of the future Emperor Charles V. But there is no other evidence of the Sieur de Berghes

* MS. Cott., Galba B III. 93. The original letter is slightly mutilated.

having been sent to England in embassy in December, 1513, though he had negotiated with Henry VIII. at Lille in the previous October. And here it is to be observed that Berghes is not only ambassador for the young prince in England, but it is distinctly indicated that he had colleagues with him in his embassy. Moreover, the extremely boyish signature attached to the document (the subscription " vostre bon mary, Charles," is all that is in his handwriting) is much more like that of a lad in his ninth year than that of one in his fourteenth. And this argument gains strength when we compare it with a signature of his after he had just completed his fifteenth year, that is to say, in his letter to Henry VIII., written on the 8th March, 1514[-15].[a] Here the handwriting is already that of a well-practised writer. Charles was evidently precocious in his handwriting, as in other things, and his signature at fifteen has a freedom and vigor about it quite beyond his years. But the words " vostre bon mary, Charles " in the letter above transcribed, though very well written, are distinctly in the hand of a young schoolboy.[b]

Ferdinand could easily afford to wait a year or two before intriguing to set aside the match. Young Henry VIII. was not yet such a skilled diplomatist as his father had been. He at once celebrated his own marriage with Ferdinand's daughter, which his father had purposely delayed, and seemed disposed, for his part, to cultivate the best relations with his father-in-law. Not many years, however, elapsed before he had bitter experience of Ferdi-

---

[a] MS. Cott. Galba B. III., 138. Calendar of Henry VIII., Vol. II., No. 234.

[b] One argument, indeed, seems to militate against the date of this letter being 1508. It is countersigned by Haneton, who was actually a member of the embassy then in England. But it is clear that it was written and prepared for signature some time before it was actually signed ; for both the month and the day of the month were originally left blank, and the " xviij " and " decembre " have been distinctly filled up in the blank spaces by another hand.

nand's perfidy as an ally when he himself was engaged in a war with France; and shortly afterwards he became well aware of the King of Arragon's intrigues to break off the marriage between Charles and Mary. There was nothing Ferdinand dreaded so much as the coming of Charles to Castile; and it was credibly said that he would be glad if the young prince died.[a] Even after the match was broken off, it was believed that he paid a pension to Margaret of Savoy to keep him in the Netherlands.[b] But he took care not to show his hand in what he did. It was no use saying anything against the marriage so long as Maximilian and the Prince's own councillors did not raise objections; and while Maximilian was co-operating with Henry in the war against France in 1513, not a syllable was uttered against it. The marriage was to take place just after the Prince had completed his fourteenth year (it was a shameful fashion, but it was the fashion, to make marriages so early), and it was more definitely fixed by a treaty made at Lille in October, 1513, to take place before the 15th May following.[c] Ferdinand himself once more expressed his assent to it[d]; and everything seemed going smoothly, although Henry very well knew that his father-in-law was secretly trying to interrupt it.[e] Nay, we find Henry VIII., when at the camp before Therouenne, granting an annuity of 20l. to a Fleming named John de Serffe until the marriage should take place.[f] But as the time drew near in 1514 the Prince's councillors began to raise objections. They disliked the disparity of age, and Maximilian was anxious about his grandson's health. When the English proposed that the marriage should be at Calais, Margaret of Savoy could not be got to

[a] Calendar of Henry VIII., Vol. I., No. 4058.
[b] Venetian Calendar, Vol. II., No. 564.
[c] Calendar, Vol. I., Nos. 4508, 4512, 4560.
[d] Ib., No. 4296, ii.   [e] Ib., No. 4328.
[f] Ib., No. 4416, and Rymer, XIII., 374.

answer. She delayed and put off as long as she could, to consult
her father the Emperor, and Maximilian, who was then in Austria,
wanted it put off at least to the *end* of May, in order (forsooth)
that he might be present.[a]

The explanation of it all was this. Ferdinand, after the death
of Isabella, depended generally on an alliance with France to secure
him in possession of Castile. Soon after the conclusion of the
league of Cambray, however, it seemed as if France was going to
win all the profits, and Ferdinand made a league with Henry VIII.
against France. An English army landed in Guipuscoa expecting
aid from Ferdinand to conquer Guienne. Their presence helped
him to obtain possession of Navarre, but he sent not a single soldier
to join them, and when he had secured his own object he made a
separate truce with Louis XII. From that time he took no pleasure in the success of the English, and his neutrality was of the
highest value to Louis. It became the policy of France to promote
the interest of Ferdinand; the chief councillors of the Prince of
Castile in the Low Countries were always French at heart, and the
Emperor Maximilian was very easily won over.

But before many months had passed, Henry was able to requite
the double-dealing alike of Ferdinand and of Maximilian. While
the Emperor was still wasting breath and energy in insincere ex-
cuses which Henry declined to accept,[b] Henry had struck the final
blow and caused Mary to renounce the marriage.[c] He had turned
the tables on his enemies, and laid the foundation of an advantageous
peace and alliance : and Mary, instead of being the bride of a boy
four years her junior, was now destined for an old man on the verge
of the grave, Louis XII.

---

[a] Calendar, Henry VIII., Vol. I., Nos. 4932, 4976, 5018, 5029, 5030.
[b] Calendar, Nos. 5041, 5126, 5152, 5290.
[c] Ib., No. 5212.

NOTE AS TO THE AGE OF THE PRINCESS MARY.

A lady's age is often a delicate subject when she is alive, but it is perplexing to find that the best authorities are contradictory centuries after she is dead. Here the Latin tract (and, of course, the English said the same) tells us, perhaps with studied ambiguity, that she was "about" eleven (*agebat circiter undecimum ætatis annum*).[a] If she was in her eleventh year she must have been born in 1497 or 1498. But the spring of 1496 is, as we shall see, the very latest date to which we can refer her birth. Her own brother Henry VIII., writing to the Pope when her engagement was broken off, tells him that she was betrothed at thirteen or when she was nearly thirteen (*cum vix annum tertium decimum attigisset*) to the Prince of Castile, then in his ninth year (*annum tunc nonum agenti*).[b] There is no doubt he gave the age of the Prince correctly, and he could have had no object in attempting to deceive the Pope as to that of his own sister, who, from what he wrote, must have been born either in 1496 or in the very end of December, 1495. This date, moreover, is confirmed by a news letter of 1st March, 1499, written from London (Calendar of Venetian Papers, Vol. I., No. 790), which says that Henry had just told the Duke of Milan's ambassador that he declined to give his daughter to the Duke, she being then three years old. Further, Erasmus in a letter to Botzheim (*Catalogus Erasmi Lucubrationum*, Basle, 1523), describes a visit that he paid to the royal household at a date which we can fix with certainty to the latter part of the year 1499, or, at latest, January, 1500. Arthur, Prince of Wales,

[a] See page 19.
[b] See the letter in Fabronio, Leonis X. Vita, 278.

was then absent, but Erasmus saw his brother Henry (afterwards
Henry VIII.), who, he says, was then nine years old (he was born
in June, 1491), Margaret (afterwards Queen of James IV.), who
was "nearly eleven" (she was born in November, 1489), Mary,
who was four, and Edmund (born in February 1499, and dead
within a year after), an infant in arms. The reckonings of
Erasmus, it is clear, are not absolutely accurate, but they are
pretty close; and they also would place Mary's birth either in
1495 or in 1496. Further, there is positive evidence that it could not
have been later than the early part of 1496, and that it was probably
in March ; for Mrs. Green discovered long ago a Privy Seal Bill
authorising a payment of 50 shillings to the child's nurse, Anne
Skeron, for a quarter's salary due at Midsummer, 11 Henry VII.
(1496), along with the usual *half yearly* payments of some other
attendants at the Court. The nurse, therefore, was probably
engaged in March (see "Lives of the Princesses," Vol. V.,
p. 2 *note*).

SOLENNES CEREMONIÆ ET TRIUMPHI.

Petri Carmeliani Carmen.

Anglia, perpetuos tibi dat rosa rubra triumphos,
    Perpetuum nomen, perpetuumque decus.
Hec tua Cesareis redolens crosa rescit in hortis.
    Atque aquilam lignis jungit utranque suis.
Septimus Henricus, sapiens Rex, regula morum,
    Celeste ingenium cum probitate tenens,
Ad tantos solus vigilans te vexit honores.
    Ergo abs te debet jure volente coli.

*Below these verses is a frontispiece (reproduced in fac-
simile opposite), filling three-quarters of the page, representing the royal arms supported by angels, with the
Tudor double rose and portcullis below.*

[*English Edition.*]

The Solempnities & triumphes doon & made
at the Spouselles and Mariage of the Kynges
doughter the Ladye Marye to the Prynce of Castile
Archeduke of Austrige.

Below this is a reproduction of the engraving described above.

B

Hoc presenti libello humili stilo edito ad faciliorem ᵃ legentium ᵇ intellectum continentur honorifica gesta, solemnes cerimonie et triumphi nuper habiti in suscipienda magna atque egregia sacratissimi principis Maximiliani Romanorum Imperatoris semper Augusti, simul et Illustrissimi ac potentissimi sui filii Karoli, Principis Castelle Archiducis Austrie legatione ad serenissimum potentissimumque principem Henricum Septimum, Anglie et Francie Regem dominumque Hybernie destinata, pro sponsalibus et matrimonio inter prefatum Illustrissimum principem Karolum et illustrissimam ac nobilissimam principem Dominam Mariam, prenominati Regis Henrici filiam charissimam cotrahendis ; Necnon Ritus et ordo in hujusmodi sponsaliorum et matrimonii celebratione adhibiti et observati, cum immenso gaudio et mutua hinc inde leticie expressione ac demostratione,ᶜ simul et hylari atque jucundo vultu, munificientia et liberalitate ipsis Oratoribus qua[m]diu in Regno Anglie immorati sunt exhibitis ac demonstratis.

HERAFTER folowe and ensue suche honourable and notable actes, solempnyties, ceremonyes and triumphes that were lately doon made and shewed, as well for the receyvynge of the great and noble Ambassade lately sent to the Kynges hyghnes frome the moost excellent Prynce his moost d[ere] and entierly beloved Brother and cousyn Themperoure and his good sone Charles the yonge Prynce of Castell, Archeduke of Austriche, for the spouselles and mariage to be had and made betwixt the said Prynce and the kynges right dere and noble doughter the Ladye Marye, nowe Pryncesse of Castyle. As also suche forme, ordre and maner as was used and had in the solempnysacion and contractynge of the sayd spouselles and mariage, with the cherefull and honourable entretaignynge of the sayd Ambassadours durynge their abode within this Reame.

ᵃ Misprinted " facmorem."   ᵇ Legetiū in original.   ᶜ Sic.

Et primum quidem, quoniam inter oratores dictorum Imperatoris
et principis Karoli ex una, et Oratores antedicti Regis Anglie
Henrici Septimi, ex altera parte, in oppido Calisie tractatus con-
ventio et conclusio perantea esset habita et determinata : non
solum pro perpetua pace et amicicia inter ipsos Imperatorem[a] et
Karolum principem ac Regem Anglie invicem ineunda et percu-
tienda, sed etiam pro jugali federe sponsaliorum et matrimonii
inter prefatos illustrissimos principes Karolum et Mariam feriendo.
Idcirco, pro pleniore complemento eorum omnium que prius conclusa et determinata in dicto oppido fuissent, prenominatus Dominus Imperator suam magnam et laudabilem legationem octo
insignium virorum ad ipsum serenissimum Regem Henricum
misit.

Quorum primus fuit dominus de Bergis,[b] ex majoribus patrie
illius dominis unus.

Secundus vero gubernator Brissie,[c] vir magni honoris et esti-
mationis.

Firste, where as here tofore a treatie, convencion and conclusion
was had and taken at y[e] towne of Calays, betwixte the kynges
Ambassadours on y[e] one partie, And Thambassadours of the said
Emperoure and yonge Prynce on the other partie, as well for a
perpetuall peax and amytie betwixt the sayde Emperoure, the
kynges highnes, and the said yonge Prynce Charles, As also for
mariage to be made betwixt the same Prynce an[d the] kynges
said right dere doughter the ladye Marye : So it is y[t] for the
perfecte accomplisshement of all suche thynges as were there passed
the sayd Emperour now of late sente his right great and honourable
Ambassade, beynge in nombre eyght parsonages :—Whereof the
firste was the lord Bargez[b] oon of the gretest lordes of those parties.
The seconde was the governour of Bresse,[c] a baron of great honour.

[a] Misprinted "Impecatore."
[b] John lord of Berghes, the Emperor's Chamberlain.
[c] Laurence de Gorrevod, governor of Bresse.

Tertius, Doctor Splonke,[a] non mediocris apud Cesaream Majestatem auctoritatis homo.

Quartus, Presidens Flandrie,[b] vir admodum prudens et litteratus ac magno in precio habitus.

Quintus, dominus Andreas de Burgo, Eques, Cesaree majestatis consiliarius, singularis sapientie doctrine et experientie Orator.

Sextus, Casselensis prepositus,[c] vir prestans, litteratus et circumspectus.

Septimus vero, Secretarius unus[d] apprime modestus ac moribus compositus.

Octavus, e Regibus Armorum Aurei Velleris unus.

Omnes sane honorifico amictu et splendido apparatu conspicui, simul et decora ac decenti familia stipati. In quorum societatem

---

The thirde doctoure Fploneke,[a] in great favour and auctorite with Themperoure. The fourth was the president of Flaundres,[b] havyng greate wysdome, lernyng and auctorite. The fyfthe Mesyr Andrea de Burgo, a knyght of Themperours Counsayll, of great wysedome, lernynge, and experience, The sixth the provost of Cassell,[c] a goodly personage, right discrete, sadde and well lerned. The seventh a secretary.[d] And y[e] cyght a kyng at armys called Toyson dore. All beyng honourably appoynted and well

---

[a] Splonke, Fploneke. The name, which was really Pflug, is misprinted both in the English and in the Latin. In Rymer it appears in one place (Vol. xiii. 228) as Pileng, and in another as Plough (238); while Wolsey, in his despatches to Henry VII., calls him Dr. Flucke. His Christian name was Sigismund, and his degree was *Doctor utriusque juris* or LL.D.

[b] Jean le Sauvaige.

[c] George de Theimscke, of whom Sir Thomas More speaks in his *Utopia* as "a man not only by learning, but also by nature, of singular eloquence, and in the laws profoundly learned ; but in reasoning and debating of matter, what by his natural wit and what by daily exercise, surely he had few fellows."

[d] This was Philip Haneton, the Emperor's first secretary and *audientiarius.—See* Rymer xiii. 230.

complures magni generosi ac domini venerunt. Inter quos[a] Dominus de Bcuers,[b] Dominus de Walleyn[c] et alii itidem ejus patrie nobilcs, numero non mediocri et valde honorifico.

Pro tanta igitur Legatione suscipienda et a littore maris usque ad Regis presentiam adducenda plurimi magnates, tum ecclesiastici tum sceulares, Equites, insuper scutiferi, ac alii nobiles innumeri, variis locis e regio mandato sunt constituti ac deputati.

Ut primum itaque oratorcs ipsi Calisiam applicuere, confestim a regio inibi deputato[d] atque ab officiariis et armigeris ejus oppidi humaniter atque honorifice sunt excepti hospitatique, et benigne ac liberaliter tractati : simul et omni eo tempore quo ibidem moram traxere pluribus muneribus donati.

Inde vero prefatus regius deputatus, vir nobilis ac strenuus, decenter apparatus et associatus, una cum ipsis oratoribus et eorum sequacibus, simul et tota illorum familia ac caterva comitante ab

---

accompanyed. In whose company there came dyverse grcat lordes, as monsyr de Bcvers[b] and monsire de Walleyn[c] and other gentylmen of those partics, a good and honourable nombre.

For the metyng and conductynge of whiche Ambassadours at and from y[e] sec syde to the kynges presence, there were at sundrye places deputed and assigned many and dyverse great Lordes, bothe spirituell and temporall. And also knyghtes, squyers and other gentyll men to a great nombre.

And firste, after that y[e] sayd Ambassadours at y[e] kynges towne of Calays had ben by the kynges deputie[d] and the hedde officers with all the Retynue there goodly receyved, honourably lodged, cherefully entertaigned and presented durynge theyr abode in the sayd towne ; the kynges sayd deputie, well appoynted and accom-

---

[a] Misprinted " quoe."

[b] Adolphe de Bourgogne, Scigneur de Bevres (Beveren).

[c] John de Berghes Seigneur de Walhain eldest son of John lord of Berghes above mentioned.

[d] Sir Gilbert Talbot.

ipso oppido Calisie, quod Caletum veteres dixere, mare trajecit atque
ad portum Dobre secundo vento applicuit : ubi Prior Ecclesie
Christi Cantuarie[a] et dominus Edwardus Ponynghs, Eques, primum
ipsos oratores exceperunt : eosque ad civitatem usque Cantuariam,
primariam Regni metropolim, honorifice adduxerunt : tradito
illis et assignato in eadem Christi ecclesia hospitio. Quo in loco
Abbas Sancti Augustini,[b] majorque et primarii ejus urbis cives,
aldermanni vulgo nuncupati, ipsos oratores salutarunt, pluribusque et
egregiis donis atque humanissimis officiis sunt eos prosecuti.
Deinde a dictis Priore et deputato Calisie ac domino Edwardo
Ponynghs aliisque multifariam nobilibus comitati, ad oppidum
Sittyngborne vocatum, atque abinde ad aliud oppidum, Darford
nuncupatum, adventarunt ; ubi comes Salopie,[c] Regie domus magnus Senescallus, necnon et Episcopus Wyngorniensis[d] ac prior
sancti Johannis,[e] simul et dominus Thomas Brandon, Ordinis Garterii Eques, ac Dominus Doctor West,[f] Regius consiliarius, egregie

---

panyed, passed with them from thense to Dovoure, where the
pryoure of Cristes Churche[a] at Caunterbury and Sir Edwarde
Ponynges receyved the sayd Ambassadours, and conductynge theym
to the Cytie of Caunterbury, lodged theym in the pryoure of Cristes
Churche lodgyng, where thabbot of saynct Augustines,[b] the Mayer
and Aldremen of that Cytie welcomed theym and gave great pre-
sentes and pleasures unto theym.

From thense they were conveyed by the sayde Pryoure, the
deputie of Calays and Sir Edwarde Ponynges well accompanyed
with dyuer [*From this point some pages in the English text are
missing.*]

[a] Thomas Goldstone.   [b] John Dygon.
[c] George Talbot, seventh Earl of Shrewsbury.
[d] John de Giglis Bishop of Worcester, Papal agent in England.
[e] Sir Thomas Docwra, prior of the Knights of St. John at Clerkenwell.
[f] Dr. Nicholas West, afterwards Bishop of Ely.

apparati, plurimis Equitibus, scutiferis et nobilibus sumptuoso habitu et equitatu associati ipsis oratoribus facti sunt obvii ; eosque ad civitatem usque Londoniarum perduxere, eisdem continue assistentes.

Porro Major[a] et Aldermanni ejus urbis simul et ordines artificum mox in unum recta linea congregati sunt ad eos oratores excipiendos, et ut eorum adventui gratificarentur ; sicque per urbem leniter adequitantes, ad preparata illis diversoria, ditissimis auleis tapetibusque et aliis ornamentis decora, ac necessariis quibusque et oportunis rebus provisa, tandem sunt adducti. Erat equidem dies quinta Decembris currente anno a Natale Christiano Milleno Quingenteno octavo, et serenissimi Regis Henrici Septimi vicesimo quarto.

Postera vero die illucescente Reverendissimus Archiepiscopus Cantuariensis,[b] Anglie Cancellarius, ac illustris comes Oxonie, Magnus Camerarius et Admirallus Anglie, ipsos oratores (Rege mandante) visitarunt salutaruntque, eorum aduentui gratulantes. Inde Consul urbis quem *majorem* vocant, simul et plebis tribuni quos vulgus *Schirifos* [c] appellat, et ipsi dictos Oratores visitarunt, egregia munera illis offerentes. Preterea mercatores Stapule et alii quamplurimi cives proxima post illam die adveniente itidem fecerunt. Cum itaque oratores ipsi biduo in primaria ipsa regni Urbe commorati essent, sese a longi itineris tum terrestris tum maritimi tedio atque incommodis susceptis reficientes, Regia majestas Palatio suo Grenwici existens ecclesiasticis ac secularibus sui regni dominis, proceribus, equitibus, scutiferis, et nobilibus ad Regale suum obsequium convocatis ac dispositis ditissime apparatis, cum aureis, videlicet, sericeisque omnifarium vestimentis, torquibus item aureis innumeris, ipsos Oratores a dicto domino Senescallo

[*Here the English text is lost.*]

---

[a] The mayor this year was Sir Stephen Jennings, merchant taylor.
[b] William Warham, Archbishop of Canterbury.
[c] The sheriffs this year were Thomas Exmewe and Richard Smith.

atque aliis primoribus regni dominis acciri associarique, et in sue
majestatis conspectum adduci jussit, per flumen Thamesim cum
magna quadam ac decora sumptuosaque regia cymba tunc nuper
fabricata, atque pro illis advehendis constituta et apparata. Quod
si enarrem fastigiosum illum ac ditissimum tanti regis et sue regie
domus apparatum, simul et honorificentissimum ordinem ad ipsos
Oratores denuo suscipiendos constitutum, difficile namque mihi
esset admodum et nimis prolixum. Nichilo tamen minus, quanto
brevius et magis compendiose potero aliquam ejus rei partem hic
inferius perstringam.

Primo namque Oratores ipsi, ut primum in regiam introissent,
per inferioris aule medium non invenustis aulcis apparate ducti
sunt, Regiis magistratibus et ministris seriatim dextra levaque con-
stitutis ; illincque primum in amenissimam porticum, quam *galeriam*
vulgo numcupamus, non multo antea ab ipso rege erectam. Mox
in magnum cubiculum regium sunt introducti ; ubi milites Regie
Custodie[a] quam plurimi affuere sumtuoso ac decenti apparatu amicti,
breviori, videlicet quisque chlamide auro et argento intexta, aureo-
que panno, veluto et sericeis cujusvis coloris adornata. Post hec
in aliud anterius cubiculum penetrarunt, quo Capitaneus regie
Custodie plurimis equitibus scutiferis ac nobilibus secum astantibus
aderat atque una cum iis puerorum Regii status magister, necnon et
ipsi pueri, quos nostri *pagios*, Galli vero *Infantes honoris* vocant,
cerulei veluti chlamidulis induti, rubeis magnis rosis ac liliis den-
sissimo auro intextis. Hic Oratores aliquantulam moram fecere,
frigus quod e flumine Thamesi contraxerant igneo secus caminos
calore pellentes.

Cum itaque rex interea temporis in suo cenaculo sub sui status
aureo tentorio maneret, Serenissimi Regis Aragonum Oratorem[b]

[*Here the English text is lost.*]

---

[a] The Knights of the Royal Body, called frequently *milites pre corpore Regis.*
[b] Rodrigo de Puebla, LL.D.

penes se a dextro latere habens, pauloque inferius ab eodem latere non parvum dominorum spiritualium, archiepiscoporum et episcoporum numerum, atque a leva manu Illustrissimum Wallie principem,[a] Cornubie ducem, ac Cestrie comitem, filium suum charissimum, una cum dominis secularibus, Ducibus et Comitibus, aliquanto inferius ab eodem latere stantibus; insuper cenaculum ipsum quantumvis latum et dimensum ingenti procerum, Dominorum, Equitum et Consiliariorum regiorum numero repletum esset; jussit Oratores predictos in suum conspectum adduci. Quibus adductis, post humilem ac debitam eorum obedientiam prestitam atque in reddendis Cesaree Majestatis litteris singularem commendationem factam. Rex nobilissimus atque omnium regum prestantissimus divinam potius quam humanam pre se ferens majestatem ac veram regie dignitatis excellentiam, humanissimis gratiosissimisque illos suscepit verbis, dicens eos bene et feliciter ad sese et suum regnum adventasse. Quo facto Oratores ad sedilia illis assignata paulum retrocessere.

Here occurs a whole page illustration, representing the King on his throne, and the President of Flanders, whose back is turned to the spectator, directly opposite to him, in the act of addressing him, the lords on either side being seated.

[a] Henry Prince of Wales, afterwards Henry VIII.

Rege sub suo aureo tentorio sedente, Oratoreque regis Aragonum ac spiritualibus dominis a dextro cornu, ut dictum est, in
declivi loco, atque Illustrissimo principe genito regio predicto
aliisque secularibus dominis eque ac pari modo a sinistra manu,
item et Oratoribus predictis ex Regis adverso consedentibus, tum
presidens Flandrie Latinam concionem propalam habuit, adventus
suorum collegarum et suiipsius causam, vimque legationis ostendens;
Cujus quidem tenor ac sensus hic fuit: quod scilicet pro extrema
manu imponenda iis cmnibus que jampridem in oppido Calisie super
amicicia et matrimonio predictis transacta et conclusa fuissent, ad
serenissimum Anglie Regem venissent a Cesarea majestate destinati.
Cui quidem concioni Reverendissimus Dominus Archiepiscopus
Cantuariensis,[a] Anglie Cancellarius, Rege mandante, dignum atque
honorificum dedit responsum.

Cum itaque hec sic acta essent Serenissimus Rex Oratores ad se

And thus, the kinges highnes beyng under his clothe of estate,
the Ambassadoure of Aragon and the lordes spirituell syttynge on
his right hande downewarde, and my lorde the Prynce with other
Lordes temporall syttynge in like wyse on the lefte hande, and the
sayd Ambassadours syttynge also directely before his grace, the
president of Flaundres purposed a proposicion contaignynge the
cause of their commynge; which was for the parfect accomplissement
of all thynges passed and concluded for the sayde amitie and Mariage
at the towne of Calays.

To which proposicion Tharchebysshop of Caunterbury chaunceller
of Englonde by the kynges commaundement made a good and
honourable answere.

This doon the kynges grace called the Ambassadours unto hym,

[a] William Warham.

accivit et illos est allocutus cum tanta verborum majestate, gravitate et facundia, ut Orator insignis atque excellens a cunctis audientibus judicatus sit et immensam sui admirationem atque incredibile gaudium omnibus qui aderant reliquerit.

Qui cum finem dicendi fecisset, urbano supra modum vultu ac regio gestu Oratores ipsos in penetralius suum et magis secretum cubiculum secum adduxit: Ubi de magnis ac secretis non parvi ponderis rebus, diu invicem sunt collocuti.

Que cum acta essent Oratores, prima illa habita audientia, Serenissimo Regi pro eo die vale facientes, Londonias sunt reversi a dominis supra recitatis honorifice reducti.

Sequenti vero luce Reverendissimi Domini, Archiepiscopus Cantuariensis[a] et Episcopus Wyntoniensis,[b] Comes Harundellie,[c] compluresque alii magni domini et consiliarii regii, Rege jubente, eosdem Oratores visitarunt, ut commissionem auctoritatemque quam a suis principibus haberent, simul et scripta que secum attulissent pro perfectione singulorum tractatuum et conclusionum

---

and famylierly entred communycacion with them upon many and goodly devyses, bryngynge theym into his Inner chambre, where after they had longe contynued and talked of and upon many great and weyghty matiers they departed for that tyme to London accompanyed with the lordes and others before wrytten.

The daye folowynge Tharchebysshoppe of Caunterbury, the Bysshop of Wynchestre, Therll of Arundell, with dyverse and many great lordes and other of the kynges counsayll by the kynges commaundement reasorted to ye sayd Ambassadours to se and examyne suche commyssions and wrytynges as they had brought with them for thaccomplisshement of all and synguler suche treaties and conclusions

---

[a] William Warham. [b] Richard Fox.
[c] Thomas Fitz-Alan, 16th Earl of Arundel.

perantea in oppido Calisie habitorum diligenter viderent et examinarent.

Que sane omnia scripta postquam visa et lecta essent, graviterque et mature, ut in tanta re conveniebat, examinata, adeo perfecta plena et integra atque effectualiter confecta reperta sunt pro dictorum amicitie et matrimonii corroboratione, ut perfectiora pleniorave aut integriora vel magis efficacia esse nullo modo possent.

Quoniam in iis primum contineretur Acceptatio et confirmatio Cesaree majestatis suo nomine pro dicta amicicia tantopere lata et ampla quantopere excogitari queat, sua sub manuali signatura et magno sigillo.

Deinde Confirmatio ejusdem Cesaree majestatis tanquam tutoris protectorisque et defensoris illustrissimi Karoli principis Castelle prenominati, insimul vigorose juncta et per ipsos Imperatorem ac principem facta sub eorumdem manualibus signaturis et sigillis.

Peramplius inter ea scripta certe obligationes et pene ipsorum Imperatoris et principis conjunctim ac divisim separatimque in

---

as were taken at the sayde towne of Calays; whiche wrytynges by good deliberation well and substantially seen, the same were founde as perfyte and effectuell as coude be devysed to be. So that for the corroboracion of y⁰ sayd amytie and mariage there can not by mannes reason more be desyred to be had.

For there is first Themperours acceptacion and confirmacion by hymselfe of y⁰ said amytie, which is as large as can be thought, under his signe and seale.

There is also a confirmacion for the sayd Emperoure as tutor and manborne of the said yonge Prynce joynctely togydre, substancially made by the sayde Emperoure and prynce with their signe manuellis and seales.

There be also obligacions and bandes of the sayd Emperoure and

solidum fuerant apposite, sese ac suos heredes, terras et subditos in magna pecuniarum summa obligantium, quam quidem summam et pecuniariam penam sint forisfacturi casu quo istud matrimonium inter Illustrissimum principem Karolum predictum et serenissimi Regis filiam predictam suum non sortiatur effectum.

Ad h̀ec eidem Illustrissime principi regie filie in patria ejusdem Illustrissimi domini principis honorifica dos est assignata, in terris videlicet et prediis ac dominiis quorum ipse princeps ad presens est pacificus possessor, atque etiam in aliis terris fundis et dominiis que illi imposterum accrescere vel quovismodo obvenire poterunt, longe largior et amplior quam aliqua Burgundie ducissa antea unquam fuerit assecuta.

Pro qua nempe dote sufficiens et idonea cautio ac fidejussio est prestita ; atque ex super habundanti terre et subditi ejusdem illustrissimi Principis Karoli de auctoritate et consensu sacratissimi Imperatoris in consimiles penas obligantur.

---

yonge prynce, aswell joynctely as a parte and severally, byndyng themself, theyr heyres, landes and subgiettes, under right great sommes of money for penalties whiche they shall forfayte in caas this mariage betwixt ye yonge prynce and the kynges doughter take not effect.

There is also an honourable dower assigned to the kynges sayd doughter in the sayd yonge Prynces landes that he is nowe possessed of and that shall in any maner wyse discende unto hym herafter, largelyer thenne ever had any duchesse of Borgoyne, and good assuraunce made for the same.

The landes countrayes and subgettes of the sayd yonge Prynce by the Emperours auctorite and assent be also bounden in lyke penalties.

Qua in re illustrissima quoque domina Margareta ducissa Sabaudie relicta, pro sua parte, eodem modo sub magnis penis est obligata.

Postremo, magnus dominorum vulgariumque populorum sub obedientia dicti principis Karoli existentium numerus pari modo in similes penas sub eorum manualibus subscriptionibus et sigillis obligatur.

Consimilique et pari modo pro dictarum rerum omnium complemento ex parte dicti domini Regis atque etiam pro perfectione matrimonii et dotis solutione a sua majestate dicte sue filie assignate et concesse pro suo connubio, que larga admodum et honorifica est, obligationes et securitates prestite sunt in eadem forma et tenore ac consimilibus penis.

Quare ex premissis constat hanc confederationem et affinitatem tanta cum maturitate, circumspectione et consilio stabilitam ac firmatam esse, et utrinque indissolubili nodo connexam, ut, nisi morte alterius horum duorum principum (quod Deus avertat) contingente,

---

The duchesse of Sauoye is also bounde in lyke wyse undre a greate penaltie for hyr parte.

And over that a great nombre of the lordes and townes under thobeissaunce of the sayd yonge Prince be semblably bounden in lyke penalties under theyr signes and seales.

And for thaccomplisshement of all the saydc matiers on the kynges partie, as well for the perfeccion of the Mariage as the payment of the dote to be yeven by his grace with his sayd doughter for hir mariage, whiche is right large and honourable, lyke bandes and suerties be made under semblable penalties.

By the premysses it is manyfeste and openne that this aliaunce and affinite is by so great afore sight and deliberacion suerly establisshed and knytte on both parties that it can not be dissolved or broken oonles it be by dethe of any of the bothe parties contrahent. Whiche

neque dissolvi neque infringi quovismodo possit aut valeat. Quod si mors etiam superveniret, nihilominus amicitia et confederatio in sua plena virtute et robore permaneret.

Certissimum est autem absque ulla prorsus hesitatione quod nusquam antea aliqua amicitia confederatiove inter aliquos alios principes inita est et conclusa, meliore animo et magis sincera mente, absque ullo fraudis seu doli vel simultatis astu interveniente, quam hec ipsa una, que inter sacratissimum Romanorum Imperatorem et serenissimum Anglie ac Francie Regem ad presens est inita et conclusa. Que haud dubie hoc tempore est nobilior confederatio, simul et grandius matrimonium quod in tota re publica Christiana existat : attentis presertim consideratisque tot regnis, patriis et regionibus quas dictus Illustrissimus princeps Karolus vero et justo titulo sibi debitas, vita comite, faventeque Altissimo, est recepturus hereditarias. Qua ex re qualis quantusve honos potestas et fortitudo dictis Imperatori, Regi et Principi atque eorum patriis, dominiis et subjectis obveniet, habentibus ex hujusmodi confederatione Ger-

---

God defende. Howe be it thamitie neuertheles shal stande in full strength and vigour.

And it is of trouth and undoubted that there was never amytie or aliaunce hertofore made aud concluded betwixt any Prynces with better wyll and mynde, without coloure or dissymulacion, then this that nowe is taken betwixt the sayde Emperour and the kynges hyghnes, whiche at this daye is the most noble aliaunce and gretest Mariage of all Christendome., consideryng the sundry and manyfolde Regions and Countrayes that the sayde yonge Prynce by right nyghe possibilite, if God sende hym lyf, shal enherite. And what honour, strengthe and commoditie shal ensue unto the sayde Emperour the kynges highnes and the yonge Prynce, theyr landes, countrayes and subgettes havynge by this aliaunce Almayne, Englonde, Castile,

maniam, Angliam, Castellam, Legionem, Granatam ac omnes inferiores Flandrie partes sibi adjunctas et innodatas, non facile judicari potest, ob multos egregios ac notabiles effectus exinde secuturos, tam ad honorem, commodum et securitatem utriusque partis quam etiam confederatorum et alligatorum suorum, necnon et eorundem regnorum, patriarum ac subditorum.

Hoc igitur pacto serenissimus Rex Anglie Henricus Septimus, pro sua celesti et incomparabili sapientia ac providentia, binas suas filias⸗ duobus maximis principibus sibi vicinis ac propinquis matrimonio locavit; Regi videlicet Scocie Illustrissimo alteram natu grandiorem,ᵃ et clarissimo principi Castelle Archiduci Austrie aliam. Quo fit ut hoc Anglie regnum cum eisdem principibus et eorum regnis dominiis ac patriis tute ac secure magnoque cum honore ac dignitate et auctoritate versetur.

Postea vero quam ea scripta perfecte ac legittime confecta reperta sunt atque hinc inde vicissim tradita et accepta, illico Rex ad castellum suum de Richmonte ᵇ pro sponsalibus et matrimonio inter prefatos illustrissimos Castelle principes Karolum et Mariam contrahendis et celebrandis movit; ad quem locum dicti Oratores

---

Lyons, Granate, and all these lowe Countrayes knytte and joyned togydres, it can not lightly be estemed; for many great and notable effectes maye and shall undoubtedly ensue thereby, aswel to the honour, weale and -suertie of both parties, theyr confederates and alies, as also to their Reames, countrayes and subgettes.

[Here occurs another gap in the English text.]

ᵃ Margaret married to James IV. of Scotland.

ᵇ The old palace at Sheen, as the place was then called, was burned down on the 21st December, 1497. It had since been rebuilt in most sumptuous fashion, and called by Henry Richmond from the title which he bore before he was King. The locality, it is needless to say, is known by that name still.

pluribus et magnis dominis ac nobilibus comitati fuerunt adducti (fuit autem sextadecima dies mensis Decembris supra nominati). Ubi non solum fuerunt omnes hospitati in separatis semotisque et disjunctis cubiculis, ditissimis auleis tapetisque et lectis supra quam credi possit apparatis, sed etiam quinque aut sex dierum spacio continuato honorificentissime tractati et applausi regio sumptu fuere.

Quod si ipsius regie domus de Richemonte decorem et ornatum atque tam Sacelli illius et magne aule quam cubiculorum preciosissimum apparatum litteris mandare velim, longum sane et mirum admodum ac perdifficile opus esset. Potissimum in recitanda pomposa et superba illorum structura ac eorum apparatu splendidissimo, simul et loci atque aeris amenitate ac salubritate, una cum artificiosissimis ac ditissimis auleis tapetisque quibus eo tempore domus ipsa fulgebat et tota erat corusca. Quibus rebus facile judicari potuit talem tamque magnificam domum toto terrarum orbe comperiri non posse ; quandoquidem terrestrem magis paradisum quam domum aliquam sive palatium representabat.

Aula siquidem ditissimis auleis auro argentoque et serico contextis undique nitebat. Qua fuit magnus et excelsus abacus vasis argenteis inauratis onustus, ferme a terra usque ad altissima laquearia erectus, miri quidem et non facile estimabilis valoris aut precii ; ubi diversi panni status aurei preciosi valde in altum erecti tendebantur.

Sacellum vero quo res divina celebratur pannis aureis ditissimis opertos parietes habuit. Altare autem Regium tot magnis sanctorum imaginibus, partim auro partim argento inaurato fabricatis, quibus preciosorum lapidum et margaritarum immensus numerus erat infixus opertum fuit ut non potuerint plures superimponi. Insuper omnia tam magna quam parva cubicula, non solum quibus Rex utitur, sed quibus defuncta Regina,[a] dum in humanis ageret, usa est, et tunc illustrissima princeps regia filia utebatur, exquisitissimis preciosis-

[*Here the English text is lost.*]

---

[a] Elizabeth of York, Queen of Henry VII., died on the 11th February, 1503.

simisque auleis auro et serico intextis fuerunt apparata cum pannis statuum aureis accomodatissimis.

Ad hec duo ampla cubicula in proprio Regis diversorio fuere preciosis mirum in modum et supra omnem fidem pannis aureis parietes opertos habentia cum ditioribus et magis preciosis lectis quam usquam visi fuerunt auro margaritis et carioribus gemmis consutis. Sed ne longior fiam quam meum fuerat institutum, hoc pulcherrimum palatium absque aliquo alio pari palatio apparatum relinquo. Hoc unum tantum adjiciens : quod neque Cresi Lidorum regis gaza, neque Mide Phrygum opes, aut Tagi Pactolive seu Padi auree arene hujus tanti Regis opibus conferri queant. Sed jam redeo ad egregiam excellentium sponsaliorum et matrimonii solennitatem, que habita est die dominica proxima, qui sextus decimus [a] ejusdem mensis antedicti fuit dies. Quo die, post solis ortum, ubi Oratores precioso amictu induti magnum Illustrissime principis domine Marie Regie filie cubiculum, preciosissime, ut antea dictum est, ornatum, et innumeris dominis ac magni honoris matronis decentissime ornatis repletum, ingressi sunt: Tum Rex a suo cubiculo secus ipsam illustrissimam dominam posito movens, illuc cum suis primoribus dominis et Consiliariis ac aliis magnatibus concessit, ipsosque Oratores placidis et benignis verbis ad pauculum temporis detinuit, donec illustrissima princeps ejus filia, ab Illustrissima Principe Wallie, Regis Aragonum et Regine Hellisabet[b] nuper Castelle genita, aliisque nobilissimis et dignissimis matronis associata ad predictum cubiculum pervenisset.

Pro declaranda autem et litteris mandanda eximia tante principis forma modestia et gravitate quam pre se tulit ac aliis laudabilibus

[*Here the English text is lost.*]

---

[a] This is an error, for the 16th December was Saturday in 1508. Of course the reading should have been *decimus septimus*. The 16th of the month has been already mentioned in the narrative (p. 17).

[b] Isabella the Catholic.

gestibus et modis tante principi pertinentibus eo tempore in illa compertis ac deprehensis, haud dubia non esset in mea potestate ullo sermone vel pagina comprehendere. Illud tamen non pretermittam quod ad formam venustatemque alterius cujusvis principis seu regine ea in etate tam tenera constitute (agebat namque circiter undecimum etatis annum) vel nulla vel rarissima admodum fieri posset comparatio. Sua namque regia humanitas et nobilis ac vere paterna quantum tenera etas patiebatur gravitas omnibus advenientibus exhibita ; habitus insuper ac gestus et bonorum morum compositio tanta fuit ut libere affirmare possim tantas tamque egregias ac certe Regias virtutes apud aliquam aliam etiam provectiorem quamcumque principem aut dominam in his tam magnis mysteriis diutius exercitatam educatamve deprehendi nusquam posse.

Quicquid enim reverentie aut humilis subjectionis, simul et gravitatis ac continentie, suo serenissimo patri debebatur ; et quicquid insuper humanitatis atque affabilitatis erat Oratoribus prestandum : id totum tanquam veterana et sapientissima princeps exhibuit.

His itaque cerimoniis sic peractis, illustrissima princeps filia Regia in altiorem locum honorifice pro illa suscipienda apparatum se recepit, ubi sola sub aureo tentorio stetit, predicta principe Wallie spacio multum inferiore permanente.

Here occurs a full page illustration representing the Princess under the gilded canopy giving her hand to lord Berghes on her right hand, the King and Prince Henry standing by. Catherine of Arragon, Princess of Wales, is on the left, and a number of spectators occupy the foreground.

Moxque aliquantula temporis intercapedine et silentio habitis, Archiepiscopus Cantuariensis,[a] Angelie Cancellarius, elegantem ac floridam habuit orationem, non modo matrimonii dignitatem et illius commendationem, sed etiam sanguinis et prosapie utriusque partis quas inter id matrimonium esset celebrandum, necnon et utrarumque progenitorum excellentiam tangentem; multiplices denique bonos effectus qui exinde sequi possent, tam pro utraque parte et earum regnis patriis et subjectis quam etiam pro universe rei publice Christiane conservatione commodo et accremento.

Qua oratione finita presidens Flandrie, unus oratorum, partem ejus orationis habite reassumens, novam atque elegantem habuit orationem, laudes amicicie matrimoniique ac uberes multifariam fructus ex iis manantes: simul et immensa atque incredibilia bona ex hujusmodi nova confederatione et affinitate secutura commemorans.

Quibus sic actis, quoniam dominus de Bergis solus auctoritate fultus erat ad id matrimonium cum dicta illustrissima principe nomine prefati illustrissimi principis Karoli contrahendum, interrogatus est si quam secretiorem facultatem aut magis specialem ultra generalia cum suis collegis mandata haberet. Qui quidem dominus commissarius et procurator, sufficienti et plena auctoritate in hac parte suffultus suam commissionem et privatam procurationem palam exhibuit atque ostendit; que distincte et aperte lecta est; per quam sufficiens et ampla potestas atque auctoritas ad contrahendum dictum matrimonium validiori et magis efficaci quo fieri posset modo per Imperatorem ac principem predictos conjunctim ac divisim fuerat illi tradita.

Qua re cognita ac perspecta causavit rex ipsum dominum de Bergis una cum aliis oratoribus ad cathedram status qua illustrissima princeps manebat appropinquare pro dictorum sponsaliorum et matrimonii celebratione ac perfectione fienda : ubi dominus ipse de

[Here the English text is lost.]

ᵃ William Warham.

Bergis, post debitas reverentias, humiliori quo fieri protuit ac
debuit modo et forma exhibitas, ostensamque maximam affectionem
et commendationem illustrissimi principis Castelle erga illam,
accipiens ipsam illustrissimam dominam per manus, recitansque
auctoritatem sibi ad contrahendum cum illa matrimonium nomine
dicti illustrissimi principis Karoli concessam, legit juxta informa-
tionem predicti presidentis verba perfectum et legittimum matrimonium per verba de presenti contrahentia. Que quidem verba
perantea in scriptis posita fuerant atque effectualiter previsa et pre-
meditata, tuneque per eundem Dominum de Bergis prolata et
ostensa, prout presidens ipse ea sibi de verbo ad verbum legit.

Post hec vero utraque manus dextra, tam Illustrissime principis
domine Marie filie regie quam ipsius domini de Bergis, invicem
juncta est et inde disjuncta, veluti in tali contractu moris est et
fieri consuevit. Illustrissima siquidem princeps tenens dictum
dominum de Bergis per dexteram manum maxima cum prudentia
et regali continentia absque ulla prorsus sibi matrimonialia verba

---

And after due reverence in moost humble maner shewed and
doon by the sayde Lord Bar[ges] with moost effectuous recommenda-
cio[n m]ade on the behalf of the Prynce of Castile, he then, takynge
my sayd lady by the hande, and eftsones declaryng thauctorite
yeven unto hym to contracte matrimony with hir for and in the
name of the sayde yonge Prynce, rehersed and uttred at the infor-
macion of the sayd presydent the wordes of parfect matrymonye
per verba de presenti whiche were before substancially devysed,
put in writyng and by the sayd lorde Barges then spoken and uttred,
lyke as the said president redde theym unto hym.

And that doon, the handes withdrawen and dysclosed as the
maner is, the Kynges sayde doughter, eftsones takyng the sayd lord
Barges by the hande, with moost sadde and pryncely countenaunce,
havynge noo maner of persone to reherse the wordes of matrymonye

recitante; perfecte pro sua parte ac distincte ipsa verba lingua Gallica longo intervallo protulit.

Que quidem verba ratione commissionis dicto domino de Bergis facte fuerant admodum prolixa: nihilo tamen minus ab ipsa Domina absque ulla prorsus animi perturbatione morave aut interruptione sunt prolata.

Que res sane complures diversosque nobiles et alios astantes atque audientes non solum mirari et obstupescere sed etiam pre nimio gaudio et cordis dulcedine in lachrimas ferme coegit irrumpere.

Postea vero quam ea verba pronunciata sunt, prefatus dominus de Bergis, illustrissimi principis Karoli predicti procurator, pro corroboratione ac confirmatione dicti contractus, non modo scriptis omnibus superinde confectis verba matrimonii continentibus per ipsum tunc ostensis se subscripsit, prout ipsa quoque illustrissima domina Maria pro sua parte fecit, Sed etiam omni cum reverentia dictam dominam est exosculatus, atque uni illius digito aureum

---

to hir utterd, spake parfittely and distinctely in the frensche tonge by a longe circunstaunce the wordes of matrimonye for hir partie, whiche by reason of the rehersall of his commission were veraye longe. Howe be it she spake the same without any basshing of countenaunce, stoppe or interrupcion therin in any behalf; whiche thyng caused dyverse and many, as wel nobles as other, then beynge present and herynge the same, not oonly to mervayle but also in suche wyse to rejoyse that for extreme cont[en]te and gladnes the terys passed out of theyr ies.

After the prolacion and utterance of whiche wordes ye sayd lord Barges, as procuratour to the sayd yonge Prynce, for corroboracion and confirmacion of the sayde contract, not oonly subscribed the wrytyng conteignynge the wordes of matrymonye by hym then uttred, lyke as my forsayed ladye dyde also for her partie, but also

annulum imposuit: proque dicti contractus sic celebrati testimonio
tabelliones duo interfuere ab utraque parte requisiti, ut de ea
re publica conficerent instrumenta: Omnesque domini ac domine et
nobiles premissa intuentes et audientes tunc ibidem instanter
sunt requisiti, quatenus de iis que in eorum presentia essent acta
testes essent et apud omnes omni tempore verum perhiberent testi-
monium. Mox tube ad classicum clangentes et innumera cujusque generis musica instrumenta increpuerunt, suosque ad longum
temporis spacium sonitus dederunt, tante rei geste tantique triumphi
gaudium et exultationem indicantes. Statimque Rex serenissimus
Dominum de Bergis, Commissarium predictum, Cesaree legationis
caput, per dextrum cubitum apprehendens, ceteris oratoribus magno
atque honorifico dominorum cetu associatis preeuntibus, ad suum
sacellum perrexit, altam et solemnem missam auditurus que eo
die ab episcopo Londoniarum [a] inibi esset celebranda.

---

the sayd lorde in reverent maner kyssed the sayd ladye Marye
and put a Ryng of golde on hir fynger, and in wyttenesse and
testymonye of the sayd contract there were two notaries there
beynge present, requyred on bothe parties to make instrumentes upon
the same. And all the lordes ladyes and nobles heryng and seyng the
premysses then and there were desyred to bere wyttenesse therunto.

This doon the Trumpettes and other Instrumentes to a great
nombre blewe and played by a good space upon theyr Instrumentes
in rejoysynge this noble Acte and triumphe.

Then immediatly the Kynges grace takyng the Lorde Bargis,
beynge pryncypall of Thambassadours by the arme, all the other
Ambassadours accompanyed with many great Lordes and nobles
goynge before his grace, passed and resorted unto his closet to here
the hyghe and solempne Masse that daye sayd by the Bysshop of
London [a] in his Chapell.

[a] Richard Fitzjames.

Cumque in suum tentorium ex purissimo panno aureo confectum se recepisset, ubi rem divinam audire assolet, Oratores in proximum contiguumque majus sacellum sunt adducti, in quo pro illis suscipiendis locus status locupletissime fuerat apparatus.

Ut vero majori misse finis est datus et psalmus *Te Deum laudamus* cum cantus jubilatione et veneratione decantatus, Oratores in aliud sacellum quo Regem reliquerant reducti sunt; Ubi rex modo ac forma supradictis prefatum dominum de Bergis secum assumens, aliis ut dictum est Oratoribus anteeuntibus, ad suum unde fuerat egressus cubiculum retroversus est, immensa Dominorum Equitum Scutiferorumque et aliorum nobilium ditissime apparatorum precedente sequenteve caterva.

Quo die Rex voluit eundem dominum de Bergis, necnon et gubernatorem Brissie secum epulari. Reliqui autem oratores ad aliud proximum contiguumque cenaculum diverterunt; ubi hono-

---

And when the Kinges grace was entred into his travers, which was of pure and fyne cloth of golde, the sayd Ambassadours were brought in to the Chapell, where was a place richely appoynted and ordeigned for theym.

And after the hyghe Masse was doon, and *Te Deum laudamus* with great rejoysyng songe, the sayd Ambassadours were eftsones broughte into the kynges closet. Where the kynges highnes in fourme and maner as before is sayd toke ye sayd Lorde Barges by the arme. And all the other Ambassadours, goynge before his grace, went and entred into his Chambre, accompanyed with a right great nombre of Lordes, Knightes, squyres, and other nobles richely appoynted.

That daye the kynges highnes caused the lorde Barges and the Governoure of Bresse to dyne with hym at his owne table, thother Ambassadours departyng to another chambre next adjoynynge, where

rificum pro illis prandium fuerat provisum. Quibuscum diversi
tum spirituales tum temporales regni Anglie domini commessati
sunt. Missa faciam in presentiarum adhibitam servicia, solemni-
tates ordinesque, lautas insuper atque exquisitas dapes: simul et
varia ac preciosa vinorum genera, necnon et auream argenteamque
inauratam supellectilem, qua regie majestati atque oratoribus eo
die est ministratum. Certissimum est autem nullum craterem
calicemve aut ciatum vel urceum sive salinum vel gutturnium,
nullamque aliam supellectilem iis mensis fuisse appositam que non
vel[a] ex perfectissimo auro denso ac lato margaritis preciosisque
gemmis ornato, aut saltem ex argento tam dense inaurato esset
fabricata ut integrum purumque aurum appareret.

Finito autem tam regali et sumptuoso prandio atque amotis
mensis, affuerunt illico diversi domini ac strenui Equites armati
ad torniamenta seu hastiludia in decus et ornamentum ac laudem
ejus solemnitatis facienda parati. Cum quibus Rex una secum

---

provysion was made for them in moost honourable maner, and there
dyned, accompanyed with dyverse of the grettest Lordes sperituall
and temporall of the Reame.

I shall not reherse what solempnitie and ordre in servyce, what
delicate and sumptuous metes, what dyversytie of pleasaunt wynes,
what plate of gold and silver gilted, the kynges grace had and was
served with that daye. But this is certayne that there was no salte,
cuppe or layer that that daye was set on the borde but it was
of fyne glod,[b] great and large, preciously garnysshed with perles
and stones, ne yet noo dische or sawcer but it was gilte and as
bryght as golde.

The dyner fynisshed, there were dyvers grete Lordes and valiaunt
knyghtes armed and preprayred[b] to just in y[e] honoure of that feest;
whiche to se the Kinges grace with the sayde Ambassadours

[a] *vel non* in orig. [b] *Sic.*

E

Oratores ducens quo lancearum concursus et ipsos armatos invicem congredientes videret, in magnam atque egregiam ejus palatii porticum, quam *galeriam* vocant, superioribus annis miro ac sumptuoso opere a se edificatam se convertit. Ibi namque patentes fenestre plurime sunt ex adverso loci quo futurus erat concursus ad tutissimum apertissimumque spectaculum accommodate. Erat autem ipsa porticus auleis tapetibusque decenter ornata, tot preterea musicis et variis ludorum instrumentis fertilis et copiosa, ut nulla ferme honesta voluptas quam quisquam optaret ibi deesset. In quem quidem locum prefata illustrissima domina Maria jam princeps Castelle, simul et illustrissima princeps Wallie, non parvo decentissimarum dominarum numero comitate, insimul spectandi gratia venerunt.

Interea milites ipsi, fortibus equis armisque et ceteris rebus ad militarem disciplinam pertinentibus abunde affluenterque et preciose provisi, tentoriis videlicet, phaleris equorum, lanceis et omnifariam bellicis instrumentis ac quibuscunque ad ipsa torniamenta conducentibus ornamentis, apparatibus insuper multis aurifabrorum artificio fabricatis, panno identidem aureo sericeoque et campanis ac nolis argenteis atque aliis multimodis preciosis et novis rebus, quas nimis longum esset recitare, ad ineundum inter sese certamen presto erant.

---

reasorted to his galarye, beynge richely hanged and appoynted ; and whyther also came my saide lady Marye Pryncesse of Castile and the Pryncesse of Wales, accompanyed with a goodly nombre of fayre Ladyes. Howe well horsed and harneissed, howe richly appoynted were the said lordes and knyghtes, with pavylyons, trappers, bardes, and other ornamentes and appareyll of goldsmyth werke, clothe of golde, silke and other ryche garnyssynge, and with belles of silver and many diverse devises, it were to longe a processe to wryte. For by the space of thre dayes these justis con-

Stabat etenim e regione loci quo congressus ille futurus erat circiter medium locus prominens et editus in faciem lati et oblongi pulpiti, tabularum structura erectus, super quo heraldi regii splendido apparatu et amictu decori, una cum regiis tubicinibus consedebant ut bellatorum ictus annotarent et eorum qualitatem tubis (ut moris est) clangentibus indicarent conscriberentque.

Ceptum est igitur inter ipsos belligeros atrox prelium, quod absque ulla intermissione, quantum lux diurna post meridiem passa est, continuis tribus diebus fuit continuatum : quolibet eorum armatorum singulo quoque die durante eo triduo cum recentiore splendidioreque ac sumptuoso magis apparatu in campum prodeunte.

Aderat ingens utriusque sexus tam nobilium quam popularium multitudo, que videndi gratia illuc confluxerat : et que fractarum lancearum fragore audito ac tubarum clangore fignum dante intellecto immensos ad celum clamores mittebat et modo uni modo alteri armato prout sua cujusque in eorum aliquem major inerat devotio majores favores voce prestabat. Pulchrum autem erat in tanto certamine innumeras lanceas armis collisas atque hinc inde confractas videre : et earum frusta in altissima usque aera sepenumero conscendere.

Eadem die dominica civitas omnis Londoniarum invicem gaudens

---

tynued, and day by day every lorde and knyght had dyversite and chaunge of appareilles every day richer than other.

And finally on the last day was also a goodly torneye, and certaynly all the sayd lordes, knyghtes and men of armes acquited theymself soo valiauntly as well in justes as tourney that they atteigned and had mervaylous great prayse, both of strayngiers and others.

The sayde sondaye nyght also in rejoysynge this feest and

his tam celeberrimis et memorandis triumphis ad omnia festivitatis
et leticie signa se convertit : nocturnos ignes pyrasque et lignorum
altas congeries succensas exigens : Organis, tympanis, lyris, citha-
risque et crotalis ac musicis quibusque instrumentis undique per-
sonantibus ; innuptis virginibus ac nuptis, pueris juvenibus et gran-
devis largos ignes circumeuntibus, choreasque sonoro ac jubilo cantu
admixtas ducentibus, dulci mero et saccaro conditis aromaticis non-
nunquam se reficientibus, donec cox intempesta ad quietem somnum-
que cunctos invitaret.

Cum autem tertius dies torniamentorum adventasset et lancearum
incursui primum data esset opera non sine pari aut non multum
absimili omnium certantium laude et gloria, tandem lanceati ipsi
lanceis despositis, fortibusque in earum locum gladiis assumptis,
fortiter ac strenue insimul dimicantes, tantum de sese experimentum
fecerunt ut non minorem in eo genere pugne quam in priore
hastarum certamine laudem apud omnes astantes sint consecuti, et
tam curialium quam advenarum et exterorum omnium judicio
magnopere fuerint commendati. Nullus etenim gladius, quantumvis forti et sincero metallo fabricatus, in ea gladiatoria pugna extitit,
qui vel non in partes confringeretur vel prorsus recurvus aut con-

---

triumphe fyres were made in diverse and many places through the
cytie of London with other demonstracions and signes of joye and
gladnesse.

Thus with dyverse and many other goodly sportes passed the
tyme by the day, and at night sumptuous bankettes were made.
Where at some tyme the kynges grace havynge the sayd Ambassadours with hym accompanyed with a goodly nombre of ladyes were
present. And at oon of yᵉ whiche Bankettes the sayde Ambassadours delyvered thre goodly and right riche tokens and Juelles to
my sayd ladye Marye, oon frome Themperoure conteignynge an
orient rubye and a large and a fayre diamonde garnysshed with

tusus vel inutilis maneret : Sicque his et aliis ludis jocisque et hones-
tissimis voluptatibus, utpote ferocium equorum taurorumve indomi-
torum atque ursorum cum ingenti mordacissimorum canum numero
certantium, dies illi jucundidatis et leticie peracti sunt. Prius
namque et aucupiis et venatibus cervorum damarumque in utroque
vivario regio quod ipsi regie domui adjacet non parvam animi
voluptatem oratores ipsi susceperant : Quorum quidem vivariorum,
quos parcos vulgus appellat, alterum innumeris mire magnitudinis
cervis, aliud vero damis, quarum nonnulle toto prorsus corpore
candent spectaculum de se prebentes est repletum.

Postquam autem nox tertie diei supervenisset sumptuose admodum private cene parate sunt, ad quas Rex nobilissimus atque
omnium regum sapientissimus et humanissimus Oratores ipsos mag-
numque cum his delectarum matronarum numerum secum adduxit;
cepitque primus conscedere,[a] deinde alios omnis ad consessum
invitare.

Quibus concessis[b] Oratores in quadam e pluribus mensa tria pul-
cherrima ac preciosissima dona illico prefate Illustrissime principi
domine Marie dono dedere; quorum unum ab sacratissimo Romanorum imperatore Maximiliano missum erat, rubeus scilicet lapis
Indicus qui a nostris *rubinus* dicitur. Magnus siquidem et pre-
ciosus simul et adamas magnis unionibus munitus.

Aliud vero ab illustrissimo principe Karolo destinatum littera
K. aurea fuit, nomen Karoli representans, preciosis adamantibus et
margaritis munitum : Quo quidem monili hec verba inscripta fuere,
videlicet, *Maria optimam partem elegit, que non auferetur ab ea.*

---

great perles, y[e] other from the yonge Prynce, which was a K. for
Karolus, garnysshed with diamondes and perles, wherin these wordes
were written : *Maria optimam partem[c] elegit, que non auferetur ab ea,*

Tertium autem ab illustrissima principe domina Margareta
Ducissa Sabaudie relicta fuerat profectum, Balagius scilicet, quem
balasion vulgus nominat, preciosis margaritis circumdatus.

His igitur cenis, tam lautis tamque opiparis ut nihil omnino
egregium quod vel terra vel freto aut flumine crescat illis ab-
fuerit, non defuerunt ludi Maurei quas *morescas* dicunt, et sal-
tantium juvenum generosa virensque propago, simul et comediarum
tragediarumque hystrionica et ludicra queque spectacula previsa sane
prius ac sumptuose preparata. Ea nocte dominus de Bergis[a] Cesaree
majestatis et illustrissimi principis Karoli predicti, jam serenissimi
Regis Anglie filii dilectissimi, instantissime petiit a Regia Majestate
et illam requisivit quatenus placeret ei dictum principem Carolum
suum filium nobilis Ordinis Garterii Equitem eligere ac creare.
Quod Rex optimo animo atque ex corde concessit, providitque
illico ut ipse princeps suus filius non solum in unum sociorum
equitum dicti Ordinis esset electus, sed etiam ut ipsa Gartera cum

---

and y[e] thirde from the duchesse of Savoye, wherein was a goodly
balas garnysshed with perles. Att whiche banket there was no
cuppe, salte ne layer but it was of fyne golde, ne yet noo plate of
vessayll but it was gilte.

There lacked no disguysynges, moriskes nor entreludes made and
appareilled in the beste and richest maner.

That nyght the lord Barges, on the behalfe and by the commaundement of Themperoure and the kynges good sone y[e] yonge Prynce,
made instant request and desyre that it wold please his grace to
elect and make the sayd Prynce knyght of his noble ordre of the
Gartier. Whereunto the Kynges grace with right herty wyll
graunted. And not oonly hath caused hym to be electid as oon of
the companyons and knyghtes of that ordre, but also entendeth

* Apparently the word *mandatu* has been omitted here.

omnibus ornamentis ad illam spectantibus brevi ad illum mitteretur.

Postremo, cum omnia negocia commissionem dictorum oratorum concernentia essent executioni mandata, quoniam dies Natalis Domini appropinquaret, Oratores ipsi, ad propria redire cupientes, a serenissimo Rege veniam abeundi supplices expostularunt.

Rex autem, quanquam magnopere cuperet eorum presentia diutius frui, et illos in dies magis ac magis sua- munificentia et liberalitate confovere, ad illorum tamen precipuam instantiam et singularem requisitionem ipsos dimisit magnis ac preciosis muneribus argentee supellectilis, necnon et levibus equis, *Obinis* nuncupatis, falconibus canibusque et pluribus aliis non injucundis donis donatos.

Postea vero quam dicti oratores tanto Regi vale fecissent et honestissima hincinde gratulationis et intime amicicie signa essent ostensa, prefatus Illustrissimus princeps Karolus, post oratorum

---

within brief tyme to sende unto the said Prince the Gartier with all other ornamentes belongynge to the sayde ordre.

And whan all matiers concernynge the commyssion of the sayd Ambassadours were accomplisshed, for asmoche as the feste of Cristmas approched, They desyred to take theyr leve of the kynges highnes to reatourned[a] to their countraye.

And albe it the kynges grace was greatly desyrous that they shuld have lenger taryed, yet at theyr instaunte poursuyte his grace despeched theym, and with mervaylous great and honourable giftes of goodly plate rewarded theym, besydes horses, hobies, hawkes, houndes, and many other goodly pleasures.

And for further confirmacion and approvyng of ye foresayd mariage, the sayd yonge prince sythens the departyng of his Ambassadours hathe sente dyverse letters subscribed with his owne

---

[a] *Sic.*

suorum legationem solutam, pro ampliore confirmatione et appro-
batione dicti Matrimonii sepe ac sepius suas litteras propria sua
manu subscriptas, tam ad Serenissimum Regem, nominando et
acceptando illum in suum bonum patrem, et ad illustrissimum
principem Henricum, filium regium, nominando et acceptando eum
in suum amantissimum fratrem, quam etiam ad ipsam Illustrissimam
dominam Mariam suam sponsam dedit, exprimans[a] ac nominans illam
suam uxorem et consociam, cum aliis gratioribus atque amicabilio-
ribus verbis quam vel scribi vel excogitari valeat.

Gaude ergo gaudio magno. Gaude, inquam, et letare, O feli-
cissima hoc tempore Anglia, atque tuo nobilissimo victoriosissi-
moque et sapientissimo supremo Regi Henrico septimo da laudem,
honorem et gratias sempiternas, quandoquidem pro sua innata prudentia, studio, ingenio, et providentia non solum in pace firma ac
quiete, tranquillitate et justicia es posita, cum summa rerum omnium

---

hande, aswell to the kynges highnes, namynge and acceptyng his grace
for his good fader, and to my lorde the Prince, takyng and callyng hym
his lovyng Brother, as also to my sayd lady Marye, expressely
callyng hir his wyfe and compayn, with other as kynde and lovyng
wordes as can be devysed to be written.

Rejoyse, Englande, and to thy mooste noble victorious and fortu-
nate soverayne lorde and Kinge yeve honoure, prayse and thankes,
by whoes hyghe wysedome, studie and provydence thou arte not
oonly set and establysshed in justice, peace, rest and tranquilite with
habundaunce of all commodities necessarye, but also thy honoure is
in suche wyse nowe enhaunced and exalted that all Christen regions
poursue unto the for aliaunce, confederacion and amytie. Thy
florisshyng redde roses be so planted and spredde in the highest
imperiall gardeyns and houses of power and honoure that by suche
spectous[a] buddes and braunches as by Goddes grace shall proceed of
them, all Christen regions shall herafter be unite and alied unto

[a] *Sic.*

tibi necessariarum copia, fertilitate et affluentia, sed etiam tuum omne decus splendor et gloria in tantum attollitur et sublimatur ut Christiana omnis religio cupiat et optet firmo tibi amicicie et confederationis nexu ac vinculo adjungi.

Tue, siquidem, tue iste redolentes rubee rose hac tempestate adeo crevere, patuleque et prominentes facte sunt, suasque radices ad altissimos usque imperiales hortos ac domos potentie et honoris extenderunt ac propagarunt, ut ex earum gemmulis et palmitibus generalis totius rei publice Christiane Pax unio et confederatio Deo favente sit proventura. Ad quem quidem honoris cumulum et dignitatis apicem ante hac nusquam potuisti attingere : Hic est nempe tuus nobilissimus supremus dominus et Rex qui te ad tam sublimem glorie statum evexit, quem non modo colere venerarique et observare jure meritoque debes, atque illi fideliter libenterque servire, verum etiam pro felici diuturnoque illius statu incolumitate et continuo successu ac quotidiano incremento tuis devotis et continuis precibus teneris Altissimum deprecari.

---

the, whiche honoure tyll now thou coudes never attaigne. This is thy noble soverayne lorde and Kyng that to so hyghe honoure hathe the avaunced. Whom thou hast cause not only to love and truely serve, but for whoes noble estate with longe and happye contynuaunce in prosperous helth thou arte specially bounde with devoute orisons contynuelly to praye.

Imprynted at London in Fletestrete at the Sygne of the George by Richarde Pynson prynter unto the Kynges noble grace.

[Colophon, as in the Latin edition. See p. 35.]

F

Petri Carmeliani De illustrissimorum principum Castelle Karoli et Marie sponsalibus Carmen.

Festa dies fulget, cunctis mortalibus Evi :
  Et solito Titan clarior orbe micat.
Vir bonus et prudens et quisquis pacis amator
  Gaudeat, et supero det pia thura deo.
Anglica Burgunde domui domus inclyta clare
  Sanguinis eterno federe juncta manet.
Ecce datur Karolo Maria speciosa puella,
  Virtute insignis, moribus atque nitens.
Septimus Henricus, Rex inclytus, est pater illi,
  Qui gemma est regum, precipuumque decus.
Regina Hellisabet mater, dum viveret, orbis
  Inter reginas floruit absque pari.
Henricus frater princeps, cui nemo secundus,
  Conspicuum toto fundit in orbe jubar.
Margareta soror Regi conjuncta potenti
  Scotorum, sapiens, pulchra, venusta, decens.
Defunctos taceo fratres simul atque sorores,
  Qui leti in celo regna beata tenent.
At Karolo genitor fuerat Rex ille Philippus,
  Quem brevis (ah nimium!) substulit hora sibi.
Cesaris Augusti spes unica, filius unus,
  Magnanimus, prestans, strenuus atque potens.
Sed Regina sibi est genitrix preclara Joanna,
  Heres regnorum non dubitata trium.
Ipse tamen tanto princeps orbate parente
  Rursus habes patrem, sorte favente novum,
Hic est Henricus, qui te et tua jura fovebit,
  Hostibus imponens fortia frena tuis.

Hic est qui pacem, sua cum vexilla movebit,
Gentibus et regnis imperitare potest.
Ast igitur laudes Supero, dominoque potenti,
Reddamus, nobis qui bona tanta dedit.
Utque salutiferum sit nobis omnibus istud
Conjugium, demus nocte dieque preces.
¶ Laus Deo.

[Colophon, a very ornamental woodcut with Richard Pynson's name and design in a central square surrounded by a square border with various figures. In the left hand at the bottom is a Virgin crowned, with the Child in her arms. On the other side, opposite, is a portrait of the princess crowned, standing erect, and behind on a lower level her father with crown and sceptre. Only the upper part of his body is seen, down to the right arm, which holds the sceptre and seems to be resting on a table.]

INDEX.

Talbot. *See* Shrewsbury
Talbot, Sir Gilbert, deputy of Calais, 5
Thames, the river, 8
Theimseke, George de, provost of
    Cassel, 4
Toison d'Or, king-at arms, 4
Tournaments, 25-29

Wales, prince of. *See* Henry
———, princess of. *See* Katharine

Walhain, John de Berghes, seigneur
    de, 5
Warham, William, archbishop of Can-
    terbury, lord chancellor, 7, 10, 11, 20
West, Dr. Nicholas (afterwards bishop
    of Ely), 6
Winchester, bishop of. *See* Fox,
    Richard
Worcester, bishop of. *See* Giglis, John
    de

PRINTED BY NICHOLS AND SONS, 25, PARLIAMENT STREET, WESTMINSTER, S.W.

A

COLLECTION OF ORIGINAL LETTERS

FROM

THE BISHOPS TO THE PRIVY COUNCIL,

1564,

WITH RETURNS OF THE JUSTICES OF THE PEACE AND OTHERS
WITHIN THEIR RESPECTIVE DIOCESES, CLASSIFIED ACCORDING
TO THEIR RELIGIOUS CONVICTIONS.

EDITED BY

MARY BATESON.

PRINTED FOR THE CAMDEN SOCIETY.

MDCCCXCIII.